Tobias Matthay

Tobias Augustus Matthay was born on 19th February 1858, in Clapham, Surrey, England. He was an English pianist, teacher and composer.

Matthay's parents originally came from northern Germany and eventually became naturalised British subjects. He studied composition at the 'Royal Academy of Music' (London) under Sir William Sterndale Bennett and Arthur Sullivan, and piano with William Dorrell and Walter Macfarren. Matthay served as a sub-professor there from 1876 to 1880, and became an assistant professor of pianoforte in 1880, before being promoted to professor in 1884.

Alongside Frederick Corder and John Blackwood McEwen (both composers and music teachers), he founded the Society of British Composers in 1905. This organisation was established with the aim of protecting the interests of British composers and to provide publication, promotion and performance opportunities. It was disbanded thirteen years later, in 1918. Matthay remained at the Royal Academy of Music until 1925, when he was forced to resign because McEwen – his former student who was then the Academy's Principal – publicly attacked his teaching.

In 1903, after over a decade of observation, analysis, and experimentation, Matthay published *The Act of Touch*, an encyclopaedic volume that influenced piano pedagogy throughout the English-speaking world. So many students were soon in quest of his insights that two years later he opened the Tobias Matthay Pianoforte School, first in Oxford Street, then in 1909 relocating to Wimpole Street, where it remained for the next thirty years. He soon became known for his teaching principles that stressed proper piano touch and analysis of arm movements. He wrote several additional books on piano technique that brought him international recognition, and in 1912 he published *Musical Interpretation*, a widely read book that analyzed the principles of effective musicianship.

Many of Matthay's pupils went on to define a school of twentieth century English pianism, including York Bowen, Myra Hess, Clifford Curzon, Moura Lympany, Eunice Norton, Lytle Powell, Irene Scharrer, Lilias Mackinnon, Guy Jonson, Vivian Langrish and Harriet Cohen. He was also the teacher of Canadian pianist Harry Dean, English composer Arnold Bax and English conductor Ernest Read.

In his private life, Matthay married Jessie (née Kennedy) in 1893, the sister of Marjory Kennedy-Fraser (the Scottish singer, composer and arranger). She sadly died in 1937.

Tobias Matthay died at his country home, High Marley, near Haslemere, on 15th December 1945. He was eighty-seven years old.

CONTENTS.

		PAGE
FOREWORD		vii
NOTE I.—The Principle of Forearm Rotation		1
NOTE II.—Arm-vibration, *etc.*		9
NOTE III.—On Pianissimo Playing		12
NOTE IV.—The Merging of the Three Species of Touch-construction,		14
NOTE V.—The Use of Bad Touch-forms		18
NOTE VI.—"Flat" *v.* "Bent" finger Tone-limits		20
NOTE VII.—The "Artificial" Legato-element		21
NOTE VIII.—The Distinction between Fore Arm and Whole Arm Weight and Movement		24
NOTE IX.—The Purpose of Arm-weight		26
NOTE X.—The Function of the Body-muscles		27
NOTE XI.—The Difference between Key-striking and True Pianoforte touch		29
NOTE XII.—The Doctrine of Key-bed Squeezing		33
NOTE XIII.—The Music-teacher *v.* the Pedant		37
NOTE XIV. The Question of Quality-variation		41
NOTE XV.—Recent Literature of the Subject		45
NOTE XVI.—On Ear-training		50
NOTE XVII.—British Piano-progress		52

SOME COMMENTARIES

ON THE TEACHING OF

PIANOFORTE TECHNIQUE

A SUPPLEMENT

TO

"THE ACT OF TOUCH" AND "FIRST PRINCIPLES"

BY

TOBIAS MATTHAY

FELLOW AND FORMERLY PROFESSOR OF THE ROYAL ACADEMY
OF MUSIC, LONDON, ETC.

NEW IMPRESSION

Copyright © 2017 Read Books Ltd.
This book is copyright and may not be
reproduced or copied in any way without
the express permission of the publisher in writing

British Library Cataloguing-in-Publication Data
A catalogue record for this book is available from the
British Library

FOREWORD.

When the "Act of Touch" was first published in 1903, many of the ideas being new and quite antagonistic to so many current fallacies, it was necessary to fence round every statement made with ample explanation and proof. Moreover, it was necessary first to bring home certain fundamental facts and principles. To prevent these main issues being obscured, many points had to be glossed over, some of which, although subsidiary to these fundamental principles, are really quite far-reaching in their bearing on Technique.

Since then, however, these ideas have become very widely accepted all over the English-speaking world. The teachings of "The Act of Touch" have also since then been rendered available for the School-room by the issue of "First Principles," of which the first twenty-six pages cover the whole technical ground—plain statements of fact being all that a student requires in the first stages. The last chapter of this primer also gives some hints as to the nature of the interpretational laws which need attention, and these have been further enlarged upon in my Lectures on Interpretation. The subsequent issue of "Relaxation Studies," with its practice-material, completed this scheme of rational *Technical* Teaching.[1]

[1] The teaching of *Interpretation* can be brought under similar rational principles, and these I have attempted to elucidate in my *Lectures* on this subject, now in the Press—"The Principles of Teaching Interpretation".

But the time is now ripe to insist a little more on some of those details previously merely glossed over, and to elucidate others which appear to have been found insufficiently clear. Hence these present Additional Notes or "Commentaries." But it must be borne in mind, that in first teaching the facts of Touch, we must still insist on the main, fundamental facts being mastered before attacking certain of these details.

For instance, the "hybrid" touches, those between *second* and *third* Species, although so important in passage-playing, should not be alluded to until the process of Touch-construction has become familiar in its fundamental aspect of three Species, and this, although the *first* Species, is but rarely required in actual performance. Once these three aspects of Touch-growth have been thoroughly grasped, it is, however, quite easy then to add that gradual and imperceptible *transition* from one to the other required in actual performance, and which will in its train bring forth the production of the "hybrids" before alluded to.

It will also be seen that the "Rotation" principle now receives far more detailed exposition than seemed desirable in 1903. Indeed, its influence on every note played should be made plain in one of the very first lessons given at the Piano, whatever touch-form is first attempted.

Allusion is also made to the revolutionary movement now at last started in Germany against the crude touch-ideas so long taught there, and with such disastrous effects. Also, in English-speaking countries there are still some who advocate "key-hitting" and "key-bed squeezing" etc., incredible although it may seem, since these ideas have been proved to be quite contrary to all mechanical law and musical success; hence the inclusion of Notes on these points, although they may appear superfluous.

Finally, let me send a word of greeting and thanks to the many thousands of my readers, who have so enthusiastically taken up my work, and are thus helping the cause of Pianistic and Musical Progress.

TOBIAS MATTHAY.

HASLEMERE, SURREY,
   August 9, 1910.

SOME COMMENTARIES

ON THE TEACHING OF

PIANOFORTE TECHNIQUE

NOTE I

THE PRINCIPLE OF FOREARM ROTATION

This matter is often so badly misunderstood, in spite of all I have said, that I feel some additional directions are here most desirable. Splendid pioneer workers[1] have published books in Germany since the publication of my "Act of Touch" in 1903, but even these are quite vague and in fact *mis-instructive* as to the function and process of the rotary-exertions of the forearm, or lower-arm, and although they prove themselves sufficiently alive to the enormous importance of this function, the true facts of the case have not been understood.

They, in fact, make so grave a blunder as to teach that the forearm rotation is to be employed to "roll" the *continuously* resting and *fully* released Weight of the *whole* arm from finger to finger! Nothing more misleading and harmful could well be conceived. Like so many others, they have only gone by "the look of the thing," and have quite failed to grasp that these same rotary exertions can

[1] Steinhausen, Breithaupt, etc.

quite well be applied without in the least showing any *movement* in consequence of such rotary application of force. Also, they seem quite to have failed to realize that the very first and most vital law of all *technique* is, that each tone must be produced as a distinct and separate muscular act (except in the solitary and rare case of "passing-on" touch) if there is to be any ease as regards Agility, or any *accuracy* musically. To "pass-on" or "roll" Weight (beyond *pp* power) from key to key, as they suggest, would indeed have the same evil influence as persistent practice (and bad practice) on the organ, or on click-instruments, or on entirely dumb keyboards. Instead of our being prompted to learn most carefully to adjust each and every touch-action to the precise requirements of each note, musically and physically, and learning to guide each key-descent with a musical purpose, instead of all this, it is certain we should acquire carelessness as regards tone-variation, an unmusical dead-level way of progressing over the keyboard, accompanied by a poor tone; and we should besides be wearing down the key-adjustments of our Piano, just as any mechanical "Piano-player" does, owing to its not relaxing the full force of its "fingers" until each note *duration* has been fully fulfilled.

The fact of the matter is, that while there is not necessarily a *change* in the rotary exertion from note to note, it is quite certain that every note we play does depend on an accurately adjusted rotary *action* (or exertion) of the forearm; it depends as much on this element as it does on the other three elements of Touch—Finger-exertion, Hand-exertion, and release of Arm-weight. There cannot be any good technique without constant care in respect of these rotary adjustments, just as there cannot be any good playing without constant alert attention to key-resistance before and during descent. In fact, insistence upon the laws of Rotation will probably correct without further trouble many of the worst faults one meets with—in the way of rigid elbow, down-pushes from the shoulder, etc., since these faults become almost impossible if we insist on freely executing constant reversals of the rotary actions and inactions. Even a beginner should never be allowed to proceed without clearly understanding the function of this rotary-adjustment, and how it applies to every finger he uses; and it is far more easy for him to learn it then, than later on, when wrong notions have been formed which are then difficult to eradicate.[1] Clearly it is impossible merely to bring the hand into its playing position (palm downwards) without the intervention of this very same rotary-action on the part of the forearm; for the natural position of our hand and arm *at rest* is with the thumb-side of the hand turned upwards. We are therefore compelled to *exert* the forearm rotarily, to bring our thumb upon the keys, and to render our hand-position "level." The exertion used is indeed a very slight one, and as we are so accustomed to it, it easily passes unnoticed, as also does the fact, that so long as we keep our hand in that position (palm downwards) so long also we must *continue* a slight rotary exertion towards the thumb—unless we support the hand on the keyboard by our little finger, etc. The often-supposed "weakness" of the little finger and fourth finger also vanishes (as I have before insisted upon) as soon as we learn to relax the rotary exertion towards the thumb which turns our hand into its level position preparatory to playing, and learn to replace *that* rotary exertion (towards the thumb) by one *towards the little finger*, when we wish to use that finger.

[1] See *Practice Card*, No. 2: "The Rotation Principle."—T. M. P. S. Press.

The supposed "weakness" of the Index finger, when that is used while the thumb sustains its note, is another of those fallacies occasioned by non-recognition of the function of Forearm rotation-adjustment, or else due to violation of the rule just given as to its application—that the direction of the rotary-exertion must always be *from* the finger that has played and *towards* the finger that is to play —so long as the "Resting" is continuous.

The fault is occasioned in this way: to use the thumb, we must exert the forearm rotarily towards it during the act of Tone-production, but instead of at once ceasing all superfluous force both of this rotary exertion and of the corresponding exertion of finger and hand, the fault made is to prolong these exertions *beyond* the moment of tone-emission, prolonging them at full stress; consequently the Index-finger has no basis for its operation and hence appears "weak." The correction obviously is to relax all that unnecessary strain, instantly sound is reached (except the slight residue to keep the key down in tenuto or legato), and to *reverse* the rotary exertion (*towards* the little finger therefore) and thus to help to "swing" the passage onwards from thumb to Index. But let us go a little further into this matter. It is true that even the most ignorant teachers, anyway of recent times, have recognized the presence of rotary changes, solely however in the form of tilting *movements* along with the thumb and little-finger, where these happen to "jostle" each other or closely succeed each other; but what has quite passed observation is the fact that rotary *exertions* (or muscular adjustments) are required practically for *every note* in *every kind of touch*, although there need not be the slightest *movement*, rotarily, to give even the slightest clue to the process enacted.

The truth is that we invariably begin by applying all the

THE PRINCIPLE OF FOREARM ROTATION.

rotation muscles—*both* the sets of forearm-twisting muscles, and that what we have to learn is to apply only the particular set required by each finger under the greatly *varying conditions* of the sequence of its entry, and that while we must learn to apply rotation in the right direction, we must also learn to eliminate (or delete) all the opposite (contrary) rotary exertions. We must relax those contrary exertions, and we must also "relax" all efforts required to make each tone, no matter from whence derived, always excepting that slight residue which comes under the heading of "the Resting."

As to the little finger and thumb, it is always clear enough in which direction we must exert the forearm, rotarily, to help them; but the matter is not always so clear as regards the remaining three fingers, since the rotary exertions employed here vary with the *order* in which these fingers are used during a continuous finger-passage. This, owing to the fact that during a finger-passage, on playing from one finger to another, the last preceding finger *acts as a pivot*, however lightly it may be rested upon—even when the act of "Resting" is at the surface-level of the keyboard, as in Staccato and in swift passages.

Thus, taking the five-finger exercise as an example, and beginning with the thumb, we shall require a slight rotary exertion to bring the hand into its playing position, with its palm downwards. Now, as the thumb should continue in contact with its key after sounding its note, the next finger in order (the Index) will require help by a rotary exertion towards the *little finger* side of the hand—and *not* towards the thumb side of the hand as would be the case were that finger (the Index) used to start a passage—and in which case there would be no "Resting" to be transferred with the thumb as pivot. The next fingers in order, the middle, ring and little fingers will, each one, require rotary help in the same direction as was required for the Index finger—that is, towards the little finger, for they all enter in the same order, with a preceding finger resting on the keyboard on the thumb side, relatively to them. We thus require a repetition of the *same* little rotary exertion for each of these four fingers—and not a "gradually increasing *tilt* towards the little finger" as some have misunderstood it. The four-finger progression back to the thumb (to complete the five-finger exercise) is accompanied by *four* little rotary actions (exertions or jerks, usually without movement) each one given towards the *thumb*-side of the hand, and applied as the ring finger, middle finger and Index come into play, respectively. Of course if the "five-finger exercise" is more complex, and not merely straight up and down, then the changes in direction of the rotary jerks must also necessarily be correspondingly complex.

In taking a scale or arpeggio, the direction of the rotary exertions are also, similarly, always in sympathy with the *order* in which the fingers come into play. Confusion may arise when the thumb is "turned under" or the fingers are "turned over," owing to the fact that the succession of the notes is straight ahead while the finger-progression is not so —the finger-progression (or order) turns back on itself and then goes on again at those turning points of the thumb or of the fingers. There will be no confusion, however, if we remember that the rule remains unaltered, and that we must apply the rotary jerks in harmony with the *order* in which the fingers succeed each other. Thus, when we turn the thumb "under," the rotation muscles tend to twist the hand and forearm down upon the thumb—although the note made by the thumb is one further on than was sounded by the preceding finger. Similarly, the finger that "passes over" the thumb is helped by a rotational jerk which tends to twist the hand down at the little-finger side of the hand—although the note itself is further on than the one played by the thumb.[1]

In the meantime, do not let us forget that we are all this while discussing the rotary *exertions* which give the fingers the basis from which to exert the force necessary to produce their notes, and that *there need not be any movement* visible except that of the finger itself. Remember, these rotary jerks do not necessarily reveal themselves to the eye as *movements* in a five-finger exercise, or in any other *finger-movement* passage. The slight rotary *vibration* which does accompany all well-executed and free "finger-passages" is however always evidence enough (to the experienced eye) of the presence of rotary freedom and muscular help rotarily.

Another thing to remember is, that if we do allow a rotary movement to accompany each note in such finger-passages, say, for the sake of *demonstrating* these rotary exertions—and it forms indeed an excellent demonstration of the process required—we must remember then, that as we do in this case make an actual rotary *movement*, we must also then each time make a return rotary movement to prepare for each next note, and that we must do this while not losing our hold upon the keyboard with the finger which we are using at that moment as a pivot—even when the "Resting" is so light as to occur at the key-surface level, as in the case of staccato finger-passages, etc.

It will now be clear why so much importance is attached to the section of my "Relaxation Studies" dealing with the elucidation of the Rotary principle.[2]

---

[1] Possibly the index-finger forms an exception to this otherwise universal rule; certainly so, when it is "turned over" far—far beyond the thumb's note: it is then best helped by reiterating the rotation towards the thumb.

[2] "Relaxation Studies"—Bosworth & Co.

After leading up to the necessity of this rotary adjustment through some simple piece or study, one should invariably begin the real study of this aspect of Technique apart from the keyboard, by taking a simple rotary movement, emphasising the matter by using a little wand or stick and striking sideways with this, rotating the hand first downwards at the thumb-side and then upwards, as shown in Section *D* of the Rotation Exercises.

Having thus obtained the idea of free rotary movement in both directions, another preparatory exercise should be taken at the keyboard itself. The thumb and the little finger in turn should be employed as the pivot upon which to rotate, while the opposite side of the hand is gently and repeatedly swung down upon the keyboard, only to its surface however —without sounding the note with the end-finger, as shown in Section *C* of the "Relaxation Studies."

Not till the learner has thus mastered freedom of motion *towards* the keyboard, will he be able to undertake the next step with success, that of making the requisite effort to sound the note *after* reaching its key—I say advisedly the "requisite effort"—for of course one is only too likely to try to sound the note while using quite a number of useless and hampering efforts.

NOTE II

ARM-VIBRATION, etc.[1]

Certain strong and yet rapid passages (both in the form of Finger-touches and Hand-touches) need some arm-weight to give the proper tonal value to them. This takes the form of a hybrid second-third Species. In such touches, the arm—the whole arm—is more or less on the point of being lapsed, and in this finely poised condition it is easily "vibrated" (owing to reaction from the key) by the rapidly repeated impetuses given by the hand and fingers. Or, the arm may actually be *slightly* released continuously, as before pointed out. For instance, the opening finger-passages of Beethoven's E flat Concerto, or the left-hand hybrid "Hand Touch" passages of the Scherzo of the E flat Sonata, Op. 31, require such "vibratory" Arm.

Without some slightly released arm-weight, *second* Species is indeed but a cold thin tone: therefore, in such "thick" finger-passages, arm-weight must be allowed to help, in spite of the fact that at such a speed a true *third* Species Touch is not possible; hence the hybrid here required. The whole arm itself, or forearm only, may be actually released continuously (although but slightly), or its necessary vibratile state may be helped by rapid reiterations of release and self-support, thus again helping as it were to "swing" the hand and fingers with the keys. *Vide* p. 27, etc., of "The Act of Touch"; also "First Principles," p. 98, and "Relaxation Studies," p. 81.

[1] Extracted from "Relaxation Studies" by kind permission of Messrs. Bosworth.

It is quite probable, that in such "vibratory" touches, slight actions of the arm muscles themselves may actually help the tone. It certainly is so in bent-finger touch, where the upper arm is of course in a "forwardly supported" state. No doubt the vibrations of the forearm seen in all such hybrid touches, and also in true "Second-species," has helped to mislead certain recent German writers [1] into the fallacy that "*all touch consists of arm-throw*" and that "Arm-weight is ever present"—a fallacy absurd enough, when we are able to recognize all the classes of touch produced by arm *lapse* (third Species), and again those exceedingly light ones sometimes required, and produced by individual finger-actions, practically quite unaided by any other action, or CHANGE in the muscular conditions of the arm and hand [2]—not to speak of the so often required *second* species, in which the arm conditions also require no *change* for the individual notes.[3]

With regard to the assertion that Weight "is ever present" in the act of touch, in one sense that is perfectly true, but not in the implied sense. Arm-weight can only be "present" *as a mass of inertia* unless the arm is separately released for each individual note, as in third species. The slight, but continuous release required for the purpose of the Legato-

[1] Steinhausen and Breithaupt.
[2] That is, "*first* Species."
[3] This sympathetic "vibration" of the arm, here in question, which arises in rapid passages, provided the arm is really perfectly "poised," has also been badly misinterpreted by these same German writers, who have been thereby led to give a most dangerous misdirection to the student, and that is, that "THE HAND SHOULD BE VIBRATED BY THE ARM!"—thus conveying a totally wrong impression of the true process required, which should *always feel, to the player*, as if the arm were vibrated purely by the reaction of the rebounding keys, and through the necessary hand-jerks required to make the tone in such touches. Set No. xviii. of my "Relaxation Studies" indicates the right impression, if studied according to the directions there given.

resting, or for "thickening," the tone in first and second species, etc., as before pointed out, does not at all come under the act of tone-production, but under the Act of Resting. In all such light first and second species, etc., where the arm has to be more or less in its state of full "self-support," one cannot indeed too strongly insist upon its being in that perfect state of "poise" which I have urged over and over again. There must always be, in such touches, such a perfect "poise" of it, that there is always plenty of "give" or *elasticity at the elbow*, so that the arm may thus be vibratorily in perfect sympathy with the fingers even in first species. But as there is here no separate release of the arm for each note—as we make no *change* in its muscular condition for each note, it is absurd to maintain that Weight here forms part of the ACT of tone-production. It can only be considered to be part of the Act of Resting.[1]

Otherwise we should also have to worry about the reactions of our body as forming part of the act of tone-production—reactions which certainly do exist more or less in every form of touch, anyway as Inertia; we should also have to consider the action and reaction of our body upon the floor, through the chair we are seated upon; and again that upon the earth, etc. This sufficiently exposes the absurdity of considering Weight as part of the *act* of tone-production when no *change* is made relatively to it before, during or after that act—an act, remember, which only lasts during the moment of Key-descent, whatever we may do afterwards, for purposes of Legato, etc.

[1] Also see Note X.

NOTE III

ON PIANISSIMO PLAYING

In speaking of "Weight-touch" as being the only means of obtaining the fullest *pp*, a touch-device should here be alluded to which greatly facilitates all soft playing. It is similar to the mechanical device employed by some pianoforte makers in their Uprights. The "soft pedal" in this case merely lifts the whole of the hammers closer to the strings, so that a considerable portion of the leverage usually available through the key is thereby nullified—*vide* p. 59, of "Act of Touch."

In playing very soft passages, similarly with our fingers we can reduce the swing of the hammer from its approximate two inches of movement to anything less, as we desire. Instead of starting the act of tone-production from the surface-level of the key, we can so carefully and "gradually" lower the key that the hammer-head is comparatively close to the string *before* we start giving it the true tone-producing swing-off. In this case we play as it were from a point in key-descent about half way down. And moreover, this key-cheating device can be applied in quick passages as well as in slow ones. It is surprising how much greater is the control thus obtained in delicate passages. No doubt gradual key-depression always has this element in it. This form of Touch requires very careful finger-control indeed. The device has been described on page 185, *Note* No. 1, and also on page 122, *Note* No. 2, "Act of Touch." The two front phalanges of the finger are here independently held with quite noticeable firmness against the key-*surfaces*,—for this slight "wedging"

ON PIANISSIMO PLAYING. 13

can be done quite well, even without depressing the keys at all. This *grip* of the key at surface-level (or slightly *below* it) is easy enough to encompass, provided we leave the whole arm (and elbow) in that perfectly poised condition here so often insisted upon—a state of the arm always required during *first* and *second* Species, and also required between each of the tone-producing impulses of third Species.

This perfect poise of the arm (and *elbow*) is very elusive—one often fancies it has been mastered, when really it has not been mastered at all. Remember, the point is, that the whole arm must be self-supported so elastically that while not the slightest arm-weight is allowed to bear upon the keyboard, the poise of the arm must be so loose and accurate that the arm is *on the very point of falling* of its own weight. If this point is thoroughly mastered, it then also becomes quite easy to give a slight degree of *continuous* arm-weight (either of the *fore* arm only or of the *whole* arm) when such is required during *natural* Legato, or in the hybrid touches elsewhere described.[1]

[1] *Vide* "Relaxation Studies," Sets II, III, VI, and VII, etc. Also the Notes Nos. II, IV, etc. of these "Commentaries."

NOTE IV

THE MERGING OF THE THREE SPECIES OF TOUCH-CONSTRUCTION

It should be thoroughly understood, that during the actual performance of Music the three foundational "Species" of touch *gradually merge one into the other*. No rigid, separating distinctions should consciously be made between them when we have actually learnt to play—except for some special point of practice.

To make such distinctions consciously during performance would inevitably lead to artificiality, and would prove rather a hindrance than a help. Analogously in painting—the three primary colours are only rarely employed in a pure and unmixed state.

Nevertheless, to gain clear ideas of the rationale of Technique (or Touch) we must first learn to understand these three forms (or species) of Touch-construction as three separate distinct things; and must, moreover, first master these distinctions sufficiently to be able to employ each as a separate touch-form. But when we have succeeded in this, we must then learn to apply them without drawing any distinctive line between them—learn to apply them in any shade or gradation of combination, between one and the next.

Thus also, we shall naturally acquire the hybrid forms which span the interval between second and third Species. For we shall find that for quick passage-work, both *piano* and *forte*, the most constantly required touch is indeed a kind of cross (or hybrid) between second and third Species. This hybrid results quite naturally, if we are always careful

THREE SPECIES OF TOUCH-CONSTRUCTION.   15

enough to attend to a most vital point connected with *second* Species, and that is, that the arm must never be held rigidly in our attempts to "hold it off" the keys, but instead, that it must be held so loosely supported, accurately balanced, or poised, as to be almost *on the point of falling of its own weight.* This has been reiterated over and over again, nevertheless readers and students are found who pass it by without noticing its vital bearing on all passage-work.[1]

Provided then, that we learn to execute our "second species" quite correctly as to this point, the arm will then be found to be *almost lying on the fingers and hand;* and we can also then at will relax it even further—either the *fore* arm only or the *whole* arm, and can thus allow *some* of the weight of the forearm, or of the whole arm to lie lightly but *continuously* on the working fingers; and the result of this will be, that the tone in such passage-work will be thickened far beyond the possibilities of the true, pure *second* Species.[2] The required degree of such extra heavy *resting* is of course naturally determined by the speed and the tone-character and tone-amount required in such passages—the higher the speed of the passage the greater can be the continuous weight thus carried and kept floating by the fingers, provided they work energetically enough to prevent its settling on the key-beds, which would of course defeat its very purpose.

Moreover, provided the arm is thus loosely poised or balanced, or is (more or less lightly) even resting continuously upon the fingers, we shall find that the arm—the forearm, or the whole arm up to the shoulder—will then be brought into a state of *sympathetic vibration* with the fingers—swinging

---

[1] See "Act of Touch," pp. 106, 112, 210 and 222, etc., and "First Principles," page 10, §35.

[2] In such touch, the weight is as it were kept floating by the quickly reiterated kicks delivered by the fingers and hands.

with them and with the keys in their movements, much in the same way that a heavy motor-car comes into sympathetic vibration with the recurrent impulses of its little engine.[1]

Here, in such quick passages, in a sense the arm does help the tone, although the arm is actually poised (or self-supported) and is not *separately* lapsed for each note as in true *third* Species; but for *slower* passages, nevertheless, we must apply this true *third* Species, with its arm-lapse separately applied for each note.

We see therefore, once again, why the properly poised arm, (or elimination of the rigidly held arm) is one of the most important laws of Technique; and the value of the resultant hybrid passage-touches also cannot be overrated—although useless for slow melodies.

But the teaching of these hybrids should not be undertaken until the distinctions between second and third Species have been thoroughly grasped, else confusion will be engendered in the student's mind.

To sum these matters up :

We must first learn how key-motion can be provoked, either by using finger-exertions alone, with loose-lying hand—"first species"; or by applying hand-exertions behind the finger for each note—"second species"; or again, for fuller and stronger passages, by the application of Arm-weight individually set free behind the finger and hand—"third species."

But having thus recognized from what components the Touch-act must be built up, we must then allow the *transitions* between these three species to supervene, and the sooner we eliminate all idea of really separating these three touchforms, the better for us musically, and technically. There

[1] Refer to No. II of these "Commentaries."

should in fact be no break, mentally, between first and third species during the playing of Music.

As to their appropriate application, I find that *first* Species itself (although necessarily studied by the learner and classified by the teacher, because of the light it sheds upon the other touch-forms) is but rarely required in actual playing. Most light agility-passages can quite well be executed by *second* Species—always provided the arm is so nicely poised as to be free to vibrate along with the finger-and-hand impulses. But with increased *tempo* we approximate towards a true *first* Species, while with decreased *tempo* we approximate towards a true *third* Species, which last *must* supervene in the case of slow passages of a cantabile nature. Moreover we find that the touch-forms most frequently required for passage-work are actually the transitional ones between *second* and *third* Species, the "hybrid" forms which bridge the gulf between these two Species; commencing for softer passages with a true second species, and as the tone increases allowing the freely poised, vibratile arm at first to relax continuously a little (either whole-arm or fore-arm only) and then gradually to break up into a true *third* Species as the *tempo* admits of it. A good example of such transition is found in the whirling, swirling passage that forms the wonderful ending of Chopin's Barcarolle;—the final notes of the last descending scale become a full *third* Species, for I interpret the passage as a great *Rubato*, ending with a huge broadening towards the final *F* sharp of the scale—and towards the following concluding octaves.[1]

---

[1] Portions of the above appeared in the author's Lectures "On the Foundations of Pianoforte Playing," first delivered in May, 1905.

NOTE V

THE USE OF BAD TOUCH-FORMS

Also, in actual performance, we sometimes have to employ what are actually *bad* touch-forms. In the Orchestra the clash of the cymbals is often thoroughly appropriate, however ugly the effect may be in itself. Thus, occasionally at the Piano, we must deliberately *force* our tone.

We should however not seek to obtain this thoroughly ugly effect by a rigid *drive forwards* of the whole arm, which merely kills all carrying power, knocks the strings out of tune, and even endangers their very existence.[1] What we should do for such rare effects, is merely to insist upon a *sudden* attack of the key in place of the usual graded attack, and the "drive" should so far as possible be given solely by the forearm, the upper-arm perhaps slightly tending forward with it, but always elastically so. In this way the tone is made very sharp in quality, without being stultified and shriekingly ugly.

Again, certain scale rushes may sometimes be appropriately executed with a forced finger-action—a similar *slight* forearm drive forcing the fingers to an exceptional effort.

One might instance the two scales in the Coda of Chopin's G minor Ballade, or those in Brahms' B minor Rhapsody. But such forced touch can only be applied provided the

[1] A "cheap and nasty" form of key *mis*-attack actually insisted upon by some teachers (?) incredible though this may seem to any one possessing any musical ear.

scale or passage does not turn back on itself. In other climax-passages the hybrid second-third Species with its freely vibrating arm must suffice, and does suffice—for instance, the passages occurring in the last three lines of Chopin's A flat Ballade.

NOTE VI

"FLAT" v. "BENT" FINGER TONE LIMITS

The remarks as to the tone-limits of "Flat" finger on page 224, on page 225 with its *Note*, and on page 228, etc., of the "Act of Touch" must not be misconstrued.

A very strong-fingered player may employ flat finger even in running passage-work requiring a very considerable amount of tone. The limit of flat-finger tone in such passage-work varies therefore with the muscular development of the player. Such passages as in the last three lines of Chopin's Ballade in A flat, just mentioned, however require "bent" finger from every player to enable the necessary climax to be obtained with sufficient brilliance.

NOTE VII

THE ARTIFICIAL LEGATO ELEMENT

A few additional words would here seem to be necessary, as the Note in the Appendix to Part III, p. 271, etc., of the "Act of Touch" does not appear to have been clear enough on this point. "Artificial" Legato, it must be understood, is a form of Legato, or Tenuto, occurring quite as often in Music as the form which, in our teaching, we have termed "Natural" Legato. Moreover, the student should proceed to the study of this artificial legato so soon as he has understood and mastered the difference between Staccato and *natural* Legato.

The difference between natural Legato and Staccato, it will be remembered, depends entirely on the difference in the Resting-weight.

In *natural* Legato we have a mere cold, pure Legato—just Legato and no more. It is obtained by *compelling* the fingers to connect each sound precisely to the next one, through the light (but sufficient) weight left *resting* upon them by the arm for this purpose—the partly released weight of the *whole* arm in flat-finger technique, and the partly released weight of the *fore* arm only in the case of bent-finger technique.

In *artificial* Legato, on the contrary, the finger and hand make the Tenuto or Legato *independently* of any release of arm-weight. In this form of Legato each finger (helped by the hand) "acts on its own"—apart from the tone-producing action; finger and hand together press very slightly upon the keybeds, and, owing to the resulting reaction, also upwards *against the arm*; they thus "jam" or wedge themselves between key and arm, very gently and subtly indeed, but nevertheless sufficiently to ensure the key being kept depressed until (owing to the timed cessation of the action of the finger and hand which provoked it) this gentle wedging (or "pressure") is allowed to vanish. The fingers are here not compelled into a general sustaining (legato-producing) action by any superimposed weight as in Natural Legato, and their action is therefore more individual, and more quickly contrastible.

To make the difference clear, take the case of the everyday experience of sitting on a chair. If the chair support is suddenly withdrawn, our legs *will be compelled* to take the weight of our body—provided our feet be properly placed as a preliminary; that is, the weight set free will compel the legs to act by reflex action, and the weight will thus take effect upon the floor, automatically! But the weight of our body can, as we know, be brought to bear upon the floor without any withdrawal of the chair; all we have to do is purposely to act against the floor with our feet and legs—as in rising from the chair. The difference is, that in the first case the action is *compelled* by the Weight set free, whereas in the second case the action against the floor is directly, from the first, at the will of the operator.

This extra, "artificial" or "pressure" Legato-element is required for all *inflections* of Legato and Tenuto, and also when we require a single note (or but few notes) of a Duration contrasting with the rest of a passage. It is applicable alike in Staccato passages, when we wish to make certain notes Legato or Tenuto, and in Legato passages, when we wish to make certain notes *more* than Legato, i. e., *Legatissimo*—that beautiful overlapping effect without which much of the charm of a *Cantabile* passage would be absent. Clearly therefore, this comparatively non-automatic "artificial" Legato-element is indeed of great consequence, musically—without it, for instance, it is useless to attempt either Bach or Chopin![1]

[1] For a clear exposition of the application of these *means* of expression, *vide* the author's Lectures on "*The Principles of Interpretation.*"

NOTE VIII

THE DISTINCTION BETWEEN FORE ARM AND WHOLE ARM WEIGHT AND MOVEMENT

When clear notions have been gained as to the presence and absence of lapsed Arm-weight, further distinctions must be insisted upon.

Certain passages which require arm-*movement* are nevertheless not ponderous enough to require *third* Species touch with the whole arm more or less released; also, passages may be too quick for *whole*-arm movement, while too slow for a natural hand-movement only. Here then naturally arises a *movement* of the *forearm* only, which thus as it were bridges over the gap between whole-arm movement and hand-movement. Such fore-arm *movement* may, when it reaches the key, take the form of a *third* Species of touch, or it may take the form of a hybrid approximating towards a *second* Species, depending upon the application or omission of upper-arm weight; that is, the *movement* may be that of the forearm alone, while this does not prevent our letting *whole*-arm Weight take effect at the last moment. For brilliant playing, movements of the forearm alone are indeed more desirable than those of the whole arm. Such fore-arm movements are also the natural accompaniment of "thrusting" or "bent" finger technique, and they actually thus colour an artist's whole performance.

In speaking of arm-weight, it should here also be pointed out that with "thrusting" touch we only can use the Weight of the *forearm* alone. For the upper arm must inevitably be *at least* in a forwardly-*supported* state when we use the thrusting or bent finger, although the upper arm may even at times be allowed to *act* forwards in addition—an exceedingly gentle action, however. If the whole limb is properly used, it will indeed always be so elastic and free, that it will *seem* to the player as if the weight of the whole arm were employed even in such "thrusting" touch. Wherefore, it is best not to call attention to this distinction between forearm and whole-arm weight until the student has thoroughly mastered the broad principle of Weight.[1]

The previous broad statements as to Legato-resting must also be modified in line with this fact,—when we use "thrusting" touch, the Resting cannot then be that of the *whole-arm* weight, it must be fore-arm weight only which is really used, possibly helped by a very slight forward action of the whole arm in strenuous passages—although it should always *feel* like "whole-arm weight."

We see however that these distinctions between Fore-arm and Upper-arm weight and movement are very important in performance. They have been thoroughly explained in connection with the "Arm-elimination tests" (Set III of "Relaxation Studies") and we again see why these should be so carefully practised.[2]

[1] Proper attention to the note-to-note rotary changes of the fore-arm will usually ensure a "free elbow" without further trouble. *See* page 3.
[2] Also see page 213, "Act of Touch," Test No. III, and Note No. 4 on that page.

NOTE IX

THE PURPOSE OF ARM-WEIGHT

The actual *purpose* of weight is often misunderstood; the incorrect notion being that the greater the weight *the quicker will this descend* with the key! That this is a totally inaccurate view the following experiment will demonstrate. Take a pencil and a poker and drop them simultaneously. You will find that both reach the ground at precisely the same moment. True, when they do reach the ground the one will have far more force to set free than the other, and no doubt that partly explains the difference we hear in tone-quality from the absence or presence of whole-arm weight, but the fact remains that the greater weight *does not move any quicker!* No, but the greater weight does permit us to *exert* our finger and hand to better advantage;— it allows us to obtain greater key-speed from the exertion of those two little levers (the finger and the hand), *because they have a better basis to work from* when arm-weight is relaxed than when it is not.

NOTE X

THE FUNCTION OF THE BODY-MUSCLES

A Manchester critic in reviewing my "Relaxation Studies" suggested that the very title of these exercises "is an exaggeration," which seems to prove that he had not even taken the trouble to read the Preface, in which I point out, that all good Technique (in the first place) depends upon *various* forms of "Relaxation." For instance:

1) On the relaxation of all effort contrary to the one required.

2) On the relaxation of the arm-supporting muscles, when Weight is required, and finally (and that had quite escaped our critic)—

3) On the prompt *relaxation* (*i.e.*, cessation) of all effort meant for tone at the very moment of its emission.

The same critic also imagines I have "not gone far enough," since I have not dwelt "on the function of the muscles of the body used in piano-playing"! Lest this should be misunderstood by others, perhaps it is as well to point out, that while the body does in a sense participate, it certainly never does so actively (by change of its muscular conditions)—except in the case of atrocious players who force their tone with sheer brute force, as if they were pushing a barrow or knocking down a bull. Indeed, there should be no action of the body at all in the act of touch itself, the body should merely participate as a huge base of dead-weight or Inertia, just as the Arm itself may be said to participate when in the "self-supported" state—for the arm then also serves merely as a mass of Inertia, and thus as a basis for the operations of the finger and hand in first and second Species of touch, and other hybrid and related touches. As the body should never participate actively in the act of touch, *i.e.*, should never change its state, muscularly, during or for that act, it would be folly to consider it *as part of our conception* of the touch-act; indeed such considerations would only hamper instead of help. Truly, the chair we are seated upon is also an intermediary in the act of touch—in a wide but unpractical sense. But this again implies the floor as a "basis." The floor demands the Earth, the Earth the Sun, and the Sun in its turn the Universe at large!

Yes, theoretically no doubt, "each movement of a grain of sand changes the centre of gravity of the Universe!"

But surely this is mere quibbling over words, and we, as teachers, have quite enough to do if we would enable our pupils to succeed in mastering the act of touch and the laws and practice of Interpretation, without worrying ourselves and our pupils with word-quibbles which do not in the least advance matters.[1]

[1] Also see last two paragraphs of *Note* II.

NOTE XI

THE DIFFERENCE BETWEEN KEY-STRIKING AND TRUE PIANO-FORTE TOUCH

After all that has been said on this subject (*vide* for instance the Note on page 96, "Act of Touch") it would seem unnecessary to allude specifically to this wild folly of the now happily exploded old German Schools, were it not that books are even now issued which try to perpetuate this primitive and childish doctrine, that touch at the Piano consists of tapping *at* the key-levers by "finger-action" or "knuckle action" alone—with all its consequent folly of extreme finger-raising and incessant exercise-practice. I found it even stated in one such "instruction" book, recently issued, that "all the great players and teachers of the past" have done so, although the fact remains that no player who ever played with any success ever did hit *at* the keys or could have done so.

Even Charles Czerny recommends that the finger should reach the key "*without any actual blow,*" and that the keys must be "*pressed down!*"[1]

Moreover, when some really *musical* teachers have mistakenly insisted upon such tapping at and hitting down of the keys, and their faulty directions have been literally obeyed, they have invariably tried to nullify the bad results of their own directions (bad tone and badly applied tone) by vehemently insisting on the pupil being "more

[1] CHARLES CZERNY, "Letters to a Young Lady on the Art of Playing"—English translation, R. Cocks & Co., 1842.

careful"—with the final result, that the pupil would then unconsciously disobey the injunction as to hitting, and would instead *carefully*——take hold of each key and "carefully" move it down with full musical purpose, and without any hitting worth mentioning!

All such fallacies arise from the "Till-Eulenspiegel" like attempt to analyse Piano touch from the look of it.

Let us re-state the points. Ample movements towards the keyboard, although unnecessary in the case of finger and hand movements, are nevertheless not to be condemned when there is time for them. They are healthy, and allow us to feel whether we are using our limbs freely or not; and in the case of arm-movements, as they permit the large inertia-mass of the arm to be brought under way before the key is reached, they also allow the arm to attain greater speed actually during key descent. But although such movement towards the key may be swift enough to *seem* like a blow to the eye-sense, yet for a musically-intended sound it never can be of that nature in reality. To enable us to *choose* aright the force which will provide the intended musically-appropriate sound, we are compelled to obey the mandates of the key itself—and, as so often already insisted upon, we must feel (consciously or unconsciously) how much force the key actually requires to provoke it into its required speed for each note. That judgment can only possibly be derived by feeling the key's resistance before and during descent—a resistance which varies with the speed at which we try to impel it. A good billiard player or a good tennis player in fact not only feels the "resistance" of his tool before contact with his ball, but also feels that of the ball *during* contact—consciously or unconsciously!

If, then, we do attend to key-movement (during its quarter of an inch) we may possibly succeed in expressing what we have musically conceived, but if we do not give such attention to the resisting and moving key, then our results will inevitably be music-less—because the act of performance has not really been prompted by our brains. And all players, past and present, who *have* succeeded in expressing themselves have had to learn this, whether they started with correct notions or incorrect ones.

The two following experiments are usually found conclusive.[1]

I): Have a light wooden hammer constructed, with a very freely working hinge in the centre of its shank. On striking at the keys with this, it will be found impossible to depress them into sound—since the hinge eliminates all trace of any "following-on" action—which is usually unconsciously given to some extent even by the supposed "key-hitters," else they would fail to sound any notes at all.

II): Place a light piece of wood (a flat ruler, etc.) across a number of keys. Now attack the wood in three ways:—

Firstly, try *really* to hit wood and keys down, but without any "following-on" action—no sound can result.

Secondly, place fingers on the wood, and push the whole down, thus sounding the notes.

It is useful in this case to cease the action so accurately as to allow the keys to rebound, and thus cause Staccato—a most instructive lesson therefore also in this sense.

Finally, come upon the piece of wood from some inches of distance, and feeling its resistance as you

[1] From my Lectures "*On the Foundations of Piano Playing.*"

reach it, do now "follow-on" and sound the notes—
and do this without stopping on the way.

This last step indeed forms the most convincing and easily
understood lesson as to what constitutes the act of tone-production, and also the *un*-act—the cessation required for—
Staccato.

Referring to "key-bed squeezing," Note on page 36, I pointed out that so far as tone-production itself is concerned (apart from musical appropriateness) all that is really necessary is, that we must make our tone before it is too late to do so. In the same way, with regard to "key-hitting," what really matters is, that we must not knock the keys down—if we desire an accurate correspondence between our musical intention and its consummation in actual sound.

Now, it is contended by some, that a slight "tap" upon the key "is helpful in certain light touches," and this, it is further contended, forms a contradiction of the rule just alluded to. There is no such contradiction, and such contention only proves that the rule has not been fully grasped.

It may be granted that a slight tap upon the key does no harm—*provided we do not knock the key down.** In light passages such slight—very slight—taps may often accompany quite good playing. The explanation of the fact, and of its good influences in such cases, is, that if we bring the finger lightly—*without* key-depressing force—upon the key in this manner, we are here supplying that free, unrestrained, movement *towards* the key which I have so much insisted upon, and which will also enable us to "follow on" with what is still more necessary, a *freely* applied exertion down *with the key*. But the thing which really matters is, that we must supply this last-named exertion in conscious or unconscious response to the resistance the key is felt to offer before and during its descent. Hence, deliberately to teach such "tapping" only serves thoroughly to mislead the student, unless his consequent wrong-doing is instantly stopped by directions to be "more careful," as already pointed out on page 29. It is therefore far better to try to eliminate all such "tapping," anyway at first.

---

* See page 18, "First Principles," etc.

NOTE XII

THE DOCTRINE OF KEY-BED SQUEEZING

It is not surprising to find veteran teachers who cannot change the habits of mind and doctrines enforced throughout a whole lifetime of misconception, but it seems incredible that younger minds can also be found thus closed to a perception of certain elementary facts!

The explanation may be the mere "callowness of youth," or the insufficient attention given to elementary Science-training in our schools, or the strange incapacity for clear reasoning so common amongst average musicians and artists.

One book has indeed recently been issued avowedly with the purpose of controverting some of the most self-evident facts of the "Act of Touch," and although the author very kindly withholds public mention of my name, he quotes copiously from my pages. Obviously this attack is based on his misunderstanding of a certain modern psychologist's works, which have evidently been scanned as superficially as my own. The phrase, "*there must be a correspondence between an emotion and its physical expression*" has been misread and perverted into meaning, that our sense of *musical continuity* demands that at the Pianoforte we must fulfil this Continuity, physically, by *continuing our tone-producing efforts throughout each phrase*, or complete *emotional statement!*—thus quite ignoring the fact that in Rhythmical Continuity and in the physical "Act of Resting" (which I have so much insisted upon) we do have such "physical correspondence" perfectly fulfilled! Such incredible mis-reasoning is of course only another proof how "a little knowledge is a dangerous thing." It would seem waste of words to allude to such mis-ideas were it not that the printed page often carries false weight with some minds.

It is only necessary to follow such mis-reasoning to its logical conclusion to prove its folly, for it would involve the dictum, that to express really strong emotion one should so strenuously force oneself unremittingly against the key-beds as to preclude one's sounding any notes beyond the first one; and in the case of unemotional music, one should touch the keyboard so lightly, as again to preclude one's sounding any notes at all!

Finally, we find it asserted by the same author that "the sounds that are silent" are the most important of all, and "telepathy" is hinted at as the solution! From this we should infer that our author must have but a vague perception of the vital importance in musical interpretation of Duration-contrasts and those of Rubato—as vague a perception of these indeed as of the laws governing Touch; and that psychology-dabbling further has warped that power of matter-of-fact analysis which can render such every-day facts of Interpretation available for practical teaching.

Proof that such would-be critics do not even take the trouble, before rushing into print, to read through the books they wish to controvert, is found in the fact that I am actually accused of wishing to "separate Technique from Interpretation," whereas I perpetually urge and re-urge that these two things must *never be separated in Practice!* In "First Principles" I even insist that "a child must never be allowed to sound so much as three notes in succession" at its first lesson, "without a musical (rhythmical) purpose in view." And again the inseparability of Technique and Interpretation is fully explained in the very first chapter of "the Act of Touch!" True, it is impossible to *analyse* mechanical facts and interpretational facts at one and the same

THE DOCTRINE OF KEY-BED SQUEEZING. 35

moment without creating a mere jumble-book. But unless we can analyse a phenomenon into its components we cannot hope to build it up by synthesis; and therefore the "Act of Touch" was devoted purely to an analysis and synthesis of the *Technique* of Tone-production, Agility and Duration, as explained also in its first chapter. To deal in addition with the other facts of Interpretation would indeed have required several volumes in place of one!

As there are also others who still regard the key-pads as tone-producers, it is worth while repeating some of the main objections to this wasting of force upon the pads under the keys. The objections are twofold, musical and mechanical;—Musically it is fatal, because if we apply to the key-bed (or pad) the force by means of which we intend to produce a sound, it follows that the force thus used will *not produce* the intended musical effect—for the force chosen will be more or less mis-spent on more firmly forcing the Piano upon the floor, instead of producing that particular *motion of the key* which would represent the mechanical consummation of our musically-intended sound.[1]   Hence, when playing under such fallacious ideas, we cannot possibly so accurately express our musical feeling as we do when we succeed in provoking the key-motions really corresponding to our musical requirements.

Again, mechanically it is fatal, because if we continue to apply the full force required for a mezzo-forte or forte *beyond* the moment of sound emission, the finger used will firmly wedge itself between the key and the superimposed levers (the hand and arm) and will by this action *disable* to that extent the subsequent fingers from doing their work—owing to the basis for their useful operation being taken from them

[1] That is, the force thus misapplied does not produce the intended effect musically.

by the earlier-used finger. That some fancy they can nevertheless influence a tone through the key-pads has a quite obvious explanation. When they purpose squeezing the key-bed they *carry the key down in a different fashion* to what they do when purposing no such folly—only their minds are too incapable of self-analysis to allow them to perceive the correct diagnosis of the process they are engaged upon.

Also, they may be misled by the fact, that we *can* squeeze the key upon its bed and nevertheless obtain quite a good tone (in the case of a slow progression) provided we do take great care to *finish making the tone we want* before commencing the futile process of squeezing flat the pads under the keys.[1]

Such foolish notions moreover usually point to a complete ignorance of the true rationale of touch, muscularly. They arise from ignorance of the fact that separate fingers cannot possibly make a tone "on their own," but that they must have a sufficiently firm BASIS for their operation, the degree of stability required from such basis depending upon the force required from the fingers, in each and every case. This basis (as made plain in the "Act of Touch" and in "First Principles") may be provided either solely by the loose-lying hand, or by the hand actively exerted, or by the inertia of the more or less loosely poised arm, or relaxed arm, or even in rare cases exerted arm.

Those whose minds are incapable of grasping such elementary mechanical facts will surely land themselves in quagmires if they venture into the arena of discussion. They should be content to accept the formulæ of those whose reasoning faculty suffices at least to cope with such quite elementary facts; facts even within the grasp of intelligent children whose minds have not been warped by misdirections.

[1] So far as the tone is concerned all that really matters is that we accomplish the making of it "early enough" during key-descent—before it is too late.

NOTE XIII

THE MUSIC-TEACHER v. THE PEDANT

While we cannot be said to teach Pianoforte playing at all unless we do instruct the pupil in the most direct way possible how to use his ears, and how to obtain from the instrument and from his muscles any and every effect he may need to enable him to express what he sees musically; obviously it remains equally impossible for him to obtain musical results unless we teach him not only Pianoforte playing but also teach him to perceive musical feeling.

And upon this point I find there is much misconception and ignorance. By "knowledge of music" is too often understood a mere passing acquaintance based upon one or two hearings of a number of musical works—the mere general sound of these, often indeed merely their names; knowledge of music, on the contrary, should really mean not only an intimate knowledge of the form and construction of musical works, but above all things a real understanding of the purpose of these works—their emotional meaning—the mood expressed in every bar of them. I find teachers of Theory imagining it is they who are teaching "Music" because they are teaching their pupils to write down such perceptions of Music as the pupils happen to have acquired. Or they think they are teaching the perception of music, by talking of the outside, the mere shell of a number of musical works, and because they teach the verbiage necessary to label the various floors (kitchens and attics and chord-furniture, etc.) comprised in great musical works, and the laws of musical grammar evident in them. I have even heard Theorists speak with contempt of those who make it their business to teach the *performance* of musical works—even incredulous that the Piano-specialist or the Voice-specialist may really be teaching MUSIC—the perception of the feeling of Music— to far more practical purpose than these very theorists!

The truth is, that teaching Music—the perception of musical-feeling—does not consist in teaching people to name glibly the various music-*substances*, nor does it consist in teaching people to write down their musical feelings, and the laws to be observed if that is to be done successfully; no, even that is no more teaching Music than is the mere teaching of Piano or Voice TECHNIQUE. True, we cannot be said to teach a composer his trade, his technique, unless we do teach him how to bring his thoughts down on paper and teach him also how to think—how to use his reasoning power to such good purpose that he will know how to build up the musical structure (of all kinds of musical substances) which shall best express his moods and feelings; just as, again, we cannot be said to teach a performer his business unless we do all the time teach him to analyse thoroughly the structure of musical works, and teach him besides how to make the instrument exactly respond to what he thus perceives in the way of structure. Nevertheless, we are not *teaching Music* at all unless we do all along make the pupil (be he embryo composer or embryo pianist) perceive better every day the spirit, the feeling, the emotional, the dramatic, the poetic, the sense of the Beautiful in Music, and all the time insist that the Technique of writing down notes, —or playing them—is purely a vehicle to express such Perceptions.

In a word, we can only learn to perceive Music, in the true sense of the term, either through the use of our own aural-analytical faculty, or through its *feeling* being made clear to us either by explanation, or through the medium of actual performance; and the greater the performer and the greater the teacher who hereby helps us young students or old students, the quicker shall we learn—not only through our reason but through our emotions.[1]

Therefore, although I have insisted upon the fact that the mere Artist has so far shown himself to be usually an exceedingly bad teacher of the technique of his art (be he performer or composer!) nevertheless it is the performer-artist who perhaps teaches us the perception of musical-feeling better than anyone else. The Joachims, Ysayes, Rubinsteins, Liszts, the Richters—yes, the Carusos, it is they who waken us up to musical perception and teach us to realize the something which music-structure is meant to convey; it is they who cultivate in the musical proletariat a better understanding of Art than they else would have. And the great Artist-teachers do precisely the same thing! It is that which we, Piano-specialists, must try to do all day long—not only must we teach the pupil to "listen,"[2] not only must we teach technique and analyse music so as to make its structure clear, from its largest to its smallest details, but we must also analyse it all, every bar, into its particular emotional moods, and make this plain to the pupil—perhaps by explanation or example, perhaps by mere gesture. It is only thus, by making the pupil perceive the *Feeling* to be expressed, that we can be said really to teach Music as well as Technique. Hence again, as teachers, not only must we try to better ourselves as actual performers, but also, we must try to make ourselves into better and better *musicians* every day—better

[1] *Vide* "Act of Touch," p. 14, ¶7; note on p. 24. Also, "Principles of Interpretation."

[2] To listen inwardly and outwardly—to judge both as to the sounds he *should* make, and those *actually appearing*.

perceivers of Music, so that we may the better light the fire of perception in our pupils' minds. You will find that the few really great teachers the world knows or has known, have all been creative artists more or less, creative artists, who from force of circumstances have had to sacrifice their own lives as composers—and to devote their lives instead to trying to make other people see and feel Music.

As regards the Theory-teachers, I gladly admit that there is a healthy spirit abroad even amongst these, especially here in England. I find there are some who do now try to teach the perception and understanding of musical-feeling—as apart from mere structure.[1] Theory-teachers, who, instead of trying to make people believe (as was so much the fashion in my young days) that learning music consists in learning to *label* the effects used in Music—the vertical combinations and the horizontal progressions, learning to string together rhythmless, hymn-tuney chunks of chord-platitudes, and in executing ceaseless repetitions of mental five-finger exercises in a by-gone lingo (which was supposed to teach us "counterpoint")—instead of this, I find that these modern teachers (real teachers therefore) do try to make the student learn to analyse music from its biggest outlines into its smallest details—precisely as the contemned "Piano-specialist" has to do all day long, if he means to get any real results from his pupil. And I find these teachers of musical Theory—and *music*-teachers—actually playing through to their pupils whole volumes of real living works, feeling that that is the only real way of provoking interest in and understanding of Music, through experience of the feelings its actual performance arouses. In fact, I am fain to say that they, also, teach Music!

[1] For instance, FREDERICK CORDER of the Royal Academy of Music.

NOTE XIV

THE QUESTION OF QUALITY-VARIATION

Lately there has once again been revived a harking-back to the old fallacy, that "Quality-contrasts are impossible at the Piano!" [1]

A few supplementary words are therefore here called for. This particular contention is a hoary old fallacy founded on a grain of truth. The fact is, if you put a key down with a stiffly held arm and too slowly to produce any sound, that the hopper then comes into action while the hammer-head is still a 16th or 32nd of an inch distant from the string, and this fact has led to the assumption that when the key *is* treated *correctly*, i.e., so as really to produce sound, the hopper will nevertheless in this case still act in the same way as under the false touch; and it is further assumed that as the remainder of the hammer's journey "must therefore be in the nature of a throw *always*, therefore nothing we can do at our end of the key can alter the character of the tone!"

Let us note, to begin with, that we here have a mere gratuitous assumption, in place of a much vaunted "scientific fact," for there is no proof, experimentally, so far, that the hammer and hopper *do* act exactly in the same way when a note is successfully sounded, as when they *fail* to sound the note under the stiff and incorrect touch-action alluded to. This is but a precarious assumption one would imagine upon which to build a quasi-scientific Touch-treatise.

[1] Dr. Steinhausen has revived it, and Breithaupt, in his second edition, has given in to him, while others have followed, like so many misled sheep.

Also, we see there is no allowance made for any *other* forthcoming explanations as to how the Quality-contrasts may arise at the hammer-end.

On the other hand, we have the incontrovertible evidence that such quality-contrasts are undoubtedly heard, *physically*, by musical people. And surely the fact that such contrasts can be heard is sufficient proof to anyone with common sense that there must be something physically corresponding to these sense-impressions—that there must be a cause for them, and also that any "Theory" or "System" which is incompatible with their existence must be a fallacious one to that extent, as not fully explaining the observed phenomena.

Although it is fully granted that Quality-contrasts and Duration-contrasts are often confused through faulty diagnosis, and that those of Duration and Quantity do much enhance those of Quality, pure and simple, nevertheless it seems incredible that any sane musician should permit himself to be persuaded by any scientist, however authoritative, that it is a mere "freak of his imagination" to fancy he hears those so clearly marked contrasts of tone, which he finds inevitably arise from the contrasts of touch-action derived from the application of "flat" (elastic) and "bent" (inelastic) finger, with their correlated arm-conditions—the absence and presence respectively of Upper-arm Weight, contrasts which are found to be available as much in *piano* passages as in *forte* passages, although more noticeable in *forte* passages.

As a matter of fact, recent experiments of my own, on the action of the hammer-shank, settle this part of the matter finally, because experimentally.

To a model Piano-action I have fixed a light but rigid metallic arm, parallel with the hammer-shank—fixed to the hinge-end of the shank but free for the rest of its length. I bring the current from the domestic electrical installation along the hammer-shank to a metallic projection fixed just under the hammer-head. By a screw-adjustment I am able to bring this projection under *the hammer* gently into contact with the further and loose end and upper edge of the *metallic arm* before mentioned, along which the current flows back to the opposite pole of the house-installation, a glow-lamp, alight, being interposed. It will now be seen that if the hammer-shank bends or "gives" during the act of touch (owing to the retarding weight of the hammer-head) that this will cause an interruption of the electric circuit—owing to the projection fixed to the hammer-end of the shank parting company with the metallic arm.

This in effect *does happen,* and we find therefore that the glow-lamp fluctuates with the differences of touch which we apply—thus proving that the hammer-shank "gives" to the weight (or inertia) of the hammer-head, causing the hammer-head to "rake" upon the string (lengthwise) more or less with the varying forms of touch; and the harmonics of the string being affected by this raking process, hence arise those differences in quality which all musical ears recognise as so important. While we may yet find other contributory causes in addition to this one, it, by itself, nevertheless suffices to account for those differences, and anyway it finally disposes of the nonsensical assertion that "quality differences are impossible through the act of touch." [1]

This error, no doubt, is greatly to be attributed to the fact that so few, comparatively, have so far learnt to *make* those touch-differences. The "elbow-into-the-key" touch —that hard, thrusting touch, with rigid elbow, so dear to

[1] The various possible hypotheses were put forward on page 93, "Act of Touch."

some of the now happily expiring German "methods," could, it is true, only give but one quality of touch, and that a most objectionable one! Also, there are to be found some ears apparently quite incapable of distinguishing between a tone that is beautiful and one that is thin or ugly. The Public itself, however, does discriminate between an artist who has some respect for his instrument and for Music, and one (?) who only makes hideous noises.

Finally, for all practical purposes it really does not signify, what we term the *results* of these touch-distinctions which the musical ear does recognise. Whether we call them quality-differences or anything else, the fact remains that we *must learn* to make these distinctions if we would be modern artists. Hence, although these Quality-contrasts were to go by some other name it would make no difference to the validity of the teachings of the "Act of Touch," for players would still have to learn to distinguish between them, and would have to learn to produce them. And it is equally inexorable that we can learn to do this only by close obedience to the laws of touch concerned, in close obedience therefore to the teachings of this work—the first rational analysis and synthesis of Pianoforte Touch, although this was overdue for well nigh two centuries!

NOTE XV

RECENT LITERATURE OF THE SUBJECT

Most of the crude technical ideas—crass wrong-doings—which had to be combated in the "Act of Touch" were originated in Germany. One is glad therefore to welcome from that quarter two important contributions to our subject,—important, inasmuch as their tendency is towards a more rational and direct form of teaching; and as they show that Germany, also, is at last becoming alive to a necessary revolution. That very thoroughness which is indeed so admirable a trait of the Teuton had here led to the most dire results, the mistaken ideas of squeezed-in hand, key-hitting, and key-bed-squeezing, "arm-force," etc., once having been there taught by some of the leading Conservatoires, these fallacies were at once adopted as unquestionable gospel, and were mercilessly hammered home, and credulously copied in other countries, including our own. Work, all too thorough, at interminable "systems" of finger-exercises, etc., was insisted upon in the forlorn hope of accidentally attaining that Agility which the teaching given directly prevented. And when, after a time, some better ideas began to dawn upon the minds of a few rare teachers, such as a vague notion of "Weight" for instance, such ideas even, though on the right path, often led to the most disastrous results.[1] The full weight of the arm was, for instance, allowed to be carried from key to key, thus actually laming and often permanently

[1] We were asked to believe by these that the weight of the finger alone, would depress the key, and that the finger would "become heavier and heavier"—if one practised long enough!

46   PIANOFORTE TECHNIQUE.

disabling many of the talented but unfortunate aspirants who worked only too well on the "systems" evolved from such half-truths.[1]

The books referred to are:—
BREITHAUPT'S "Die Natürliche Klaviertechnik" and DR. STEINHAUSEN'S "Klaviertechnik," and these will undoubtedly help forward better ideas. Although both books were published subsequently to "The Act of Touch" this, evidently, was unknown anyway to Breithaupt, and it is all the more gratifying to find so much coincidence in the conclusions on many of the main points, such as the element of Arm-weight, Rotation, etc.

Breithaupt, a musician and journalist, is delightfully strong in his unmitigated denouncement of the now exploded German ideas of touch by "finger-power" alone, and mere exercise "methods." His touch-ideas he seems to have based mainly on the "Deppe-Caland" teachings of Freedom and Weight. But he is not very definite in actual directions, and fails owing to his attempting to solve the touch-problems through the eye. Hence we find, after all, much insistence on mere Movements in place of definite instructions

[1] To instance a concrete case, one of many sad ones. An enthusiastic, musical, persevering young player, with much naturally-gained Agility, must needs go to Germany—owing to the reputation which "Leipzig" had formerly made for herself during Mendelssohn's career there. During two years' hard study, he found his powers of Agility gradually waning, his arms growing so painful that at last medical advice was sought. One expert after another failed, however, to diagnose his case aright, but as all agreed that "all practice must be stopped," he had, miserably, to give up all hope of the artistic career for which he was so well fitted. It was after some ten years spent without daring to resume practice, that he came under my observation, and it was then found that the supposed "fell disease" was merely "weight" wrongly applied!—His teacher had instructed him to use that as fully as possible, but had wrecked his pupil's career by failing to instruct him to apply it only during the moment of key-descent; and with such a heavy arm as he had, can one wonder at the sad result?

muscularly—Movement being still insisted upon as the Cause, instead of merely the Result of the proper Touch *actions* muscularly. And although he gives my work some very appreciative remarks in his Second Edition (1905) the limit of his advancement is proved by his confessing himself "unable to follow" some of the obvious explanations.[1]

Steinhausen's work is of quite a different calibre. The work of a layman, musically (he is I believe a Doctor of Physiology and Science) it is splendidly definite, clear, and logical so far as it goes. The clearly-put information as to the key itself might indeed serve as a free translation of my Part II, and his condemnations of the now out-of-date Finger-touch and Finger-practice "methods" (still so rampant in Germany) are even stronger than Breithaupt's, and form delightful reading. Also, if my work was unknown to him, it is very gratifying to find that he was led to so many conclusions in harmony with mine, seeing that he had approached the problems purely from the scientific and physiological side.

Unfortunately his work, also, is marred by some very serious defects. He starts by denying the possibility of Quality-variations (vide *Note*, No. XIV), and while he does good work in insisting (as I did in the earlier work) on Arm-weight and Fore-arm Rotation, he makes the grave blunder of concluding that *all* touch is a sort of cross between Touch by Arm-weight and Arm-force, and is always more or less "arm-throw" whatever the passage![2] Moreover, he also, like Breithaupt, fails to see that full Weight must never be applied except *during* the act itself of tone-production, if Music and limbs are to be safe.

Then owing to his obviously having had to rely on his

[1] "Die Natürliche Klaviertechnik," second edition (1905), page 374, etc.

[2] Arm-*swing* would be a better term, and would in fact prove as suggestive of the right action, as "throw" is of the wrong one.

eye as to the muscular means adopted by the artist in producing his effects, here again, we still have that old-fashioned insistence upon mere Movements and Motions, and very little information as to the muscular changes required. He indeed, goes so far as to deny that it is "possible" to analyse the muscular conditions, which, to say the least of it, is a distinctly un-scientific and feeble attitude to take up—but quite logical, seeing that he, as a layman, could not be expected to be able to analyse the touch-actions except by outside, visual impressions.

To attempt to discover the rationale of Piano-technique or Touch-variety purely by eye-evidence—solely by watching the *resultant* Movements exhibited by a successful player—is just about as foolish as hoping to understand, say, the mechanism of a steam-locomotive, or other motor, from the visible movements it exhibits. The would-be Scientist would as likely as not conclude that the driver's turning of a handle is the actual "power" which "causes" the wheels to rotate, and that these push the pistons in and out of the cylinders and thus "cause" steam to be pushed out of the funnel—as a child once put it! True, the rotations of the wheels form *part of the phenomenon,* and they transmit the power of the engine, but such rotations are no more the "cause" of the locomotion, than Touch-movements are the "cause" of Touch in its millions of manifestations! In fact, it would not at all be considered "scientific" to assert "no doubt there is here a complex machinery which assists these wheels to move, but it is too difficult to understand!" But, it is just as unscientific to dismiss (as Steinhausen does) the "possibility" of analysing the muscular actions and inactions of Touch because they are mostly invisible. As a matter of fact, they are quite easy to diagnose, if we try to do so "from within" and not from the mere outside appearances upon which Dr. Steinhausen has apparently had to rely.

But both these pioneer works will do good in Germany, where they were so badly needed, as they will pave the way for more accurate knowledge and better technical teaching there, and thus perhaps allow Germany to regain the ground lost during the last quarter or half century.

NOTE XVI

ON EAR-TRAINING

Perhaps the most striking, the most glaring fault made by those who try to use a musical instrument is one which is never or but rarely committed when learning anything else. In trying to learn anything else, at least the effort is made to use *the requisite sense-organ*, but not so in Music!

There are indeed few aspirants who, when they try to draw a picture or to write a sentence or two, do not at least turn their eyes upon the work in hand, even if they do forget (often enough) to use their imagination in the first place. Even a carpenter or a bricklayer does usually try to *see* what he is doing. Yet we find that most musical aspirants will persist in trying to use any *other* sense-organ but the particular one which, alone, will really help them. And this mistake is persisted in, in spite of the advantage we here have, that it is not possible to *shut* our physical ears as we can shut our physical eyes. Moreover, it is not realized that the mere fact of receiving light-impressions or aural-impressions does not necessarily imply that we are *using* those organs at all; and that really *to perceive* anything through those organs we must apply our consciousness through them. True, we cannot prevent masses of sound reaching our ear-organ, but the difference between merely *hearing* and really *listening* is vast—it is the difference between receiving a general impression of a sound-fog driven in upon us, and receiving the clear-cut impression of true *perception* which results when we use our outer ears, consciously, so that we may *really* hear—really notice—what we are doing, how each note does sound; in other words, so that we may realize what is the actual result of the efforts we are applying to the instrument.[1] Nevertheless, unless we do make this effort every moment we are playing or practising, we are indeed groping in the dark, just as much as we should be, if we turned our eyes away from the painting or drawing we are trying to execute.

There has been much talk lately of "ear-training", some of it most commendable, but much of it perhaps futile. . . . It certainly is futile, if separated from the actual teaching of Music, and if a teacher allows a pupil to proceed *for one moment* without any manifest attempt accurately to hear and notice what he is doing—that is, without his accurately *analysing the sounds* he is making.

No true music-lesson, indeed, can ever be given without true "ear-training" being enforced by the teacher every moment of the lesson-hour. Unless that is fully realized there can be but little progress musically.

[1] *Vide* "Act of Touch" on "Listening," pp. 32, 41, etc. Also, "The Principles of Interpretation."

NOTE XVII

BRITISH PIANO PROGRESS [1]

What have the last two decades done for our progress, pianistically? They have, indeed, left their mark in this country—a progress particularly striking both as regards piano-playing and piano-composing; a progress which must be attributed in the first place, to the great advance made in teaching.

Twenty years ago no British aspirant felt safe unless he had finished his schooling abroad, but all this, happily, is now past history. Germany is no longer the fetish-word it then was, musically. True, we have to thank Germany for most of the greatest music ever written—but, also, we have to thank her, pianistically, for much of the very worst teaching, to instance only the interminable exercise-grinding and monumental blunders of some of her "Schools" and "Methods"—methods which were accepted here and in America as undeniable gospel. But the awakening in this respect has now at last also come to Germany herself, and several healthily revolutionary writers are now trying, with trenchant pen to bring her to her senses and "up-to-date," in the way of more common-sense teaching methods not dissimilar to those already so well established in our country. Our progress is proved in many ways. The examination room affords striking evidence in this respect, and it points to an immense stride forward in teaching generally throughout the country. Real great talents are,

[1] This was the author's contribution to the 1,000th number of "Musical News," April 30, 1910.

perhaps, not more frequently to be met with now than formerly. The advance is in the general level attained; and although we still meet with appalling instances of mis-training and non-training, yet such depths of musical depravity are no longer found to be the rule, as was the case twenty years ago—even the bottommost level is far better, technically and musically. Long-cherished fallacies have been thrown overboard, and it is now comparatively rare to find poor students giving passages with more notes obliterated than sounded, simply owing to their having been mistaught to hit at the keys, or else to press them down as hard as possible—not to speak of all the other possible forms of false key-treatment so rampant only a few years ago. And, as a corollary, we find that the talented ones do also commensurately attain a far higher level. Indeed, comparing the average English piano-student with the average German student, we must pronounce England to have won the day—for the present.

But it was not only bad teaching which cramped us before. When the foreigner proved his immense superiority over ourselves, we were content to try to excuse our own feebleness by ascribing his success to "better talent." Since then it has dawned upon us that while real "talent" is always comparatively rare, it is *no rarer here* than elsewhere, and that our failure mostly arose from sheer apathy, want of real trying, real earnestness, real persistence in our work, and it is the far more strenuous and determined work done in recent years which has so greatly contributed to our success.

But the lesson must still be driven home. How often do we still find our artists, young and old, going before the public with chamber works only half rehearsed, trusting that the public will not notice the deficiencies! Here the foreigner, with his fine self-respect, is still a great reproach to us.

Finally, we come to the most striking feature of our progress pianistically. Two decades ago, it is true, we could point to pianists of the first rank who were British-born; to mention only three names, we had Eugen d'Albert (MacCulloch) the greatest of all Beethoven players, also Leonard Borwick, and Fanny Davies. But since then we have gone further, for we now have quite a number of notable pianists, with reputations gained here and abroad, who are not only British-born, but solely British-*trained*, or who have received their *final* training in this country;[1] and, alongside of these fine artists is springing up a school of British-trained composers for the instrument, who also promise quite to hold their own with the foreigner, because of their delightfully strong, virile and original work. This is a new departure of which we, as a nation, may well feel proud.[2]

Here we have indeed, the most hopeful sign, musically, in this country. Owing to the real success of the British-born and British-bred pianist and composer, a revulsion in public feeling is clearly manifesting itself. No longer do

---

[1] I must refrain from mentioning names here, since many of these, I am glad to say, have been my own pupils.

[2] To mention only a few of the most prominent names from this young rising School of British *Piano* writers, we have:—BENJAMIN DALE, with his wonderful Sonata, two Suites for Viola and Piano, "Night Fancies," etc.; YORK BOWEN (two Miniature Suites, three Concertos, two Sonatas for Viola and Piano, Violin Suite, etc.); JAMES FRISKIN, Quintette for Piano and Strings, Quintette in C and Fantasy-Trio for Piano and Strings, Ballade for Piano, etc.; PAUL CORDER, Preludes, etc.; FELIX SWINSTEAD, Prelude in D, and Seven Preludes, etc.; ARNOLD BAX, Waltz, etc.; FRANK BRIDGE, Fantasy-Trio for Piano and Strings, etc.; CYRIL SCOTT, JOSEPH HOLBROOKE, HARRY FARJEON, etc. Amongst this "young" school might also be counted J. B. MCEWEN, with his fine Sonata, Sketches, etc.; but the list might easily be extended still further.

our public and its leaders contemn a composer or artist, merely because he is British; and although, with true British false modesty, we are still diffident about praising our own kith and kin, repeated experience has so driven home the fact that the home article is as good (and mostly much better) than the foreign product, that our public is now fain to welcome the British artist almost, if not quite, as warmly as he is welcomed by Continental audiences.

It is a good piece of work accomplished in two decades, and it justifies an encouraging outlook for the future of British Art.

EDUCATIONAL WORKS FOR PIANOFORTE BY
TOBIAS MATTHAY

With 22 Illustrations. 8vo, pp. xlii + 328. 10s. 6d.

THE ACT OF TOUCH
IN ALL ITS DIVERSITY.

Musical Times says:

"When Mr. Tobias Matthay first published his work, 'The Act of Touch, in 1903, it was received with very mixed feelings by the musical profession. Many scoffed at the mere fact that an acknowledged expert required some 300 pages of closely printed matter to explain how to play the pianoforte; others regarded the book as **a 'one man's fad,'** which would have its day and be gone; others indignantly denied that anything could be wrong with existing methods, which had produced a Liszt, a Rubinstein, a Madame Schumann. But the wise, even if unable to grasp a tithe of the new gospel at first, recognised the fact that here was something giving food for thought and experiment.

"And now? The 'one-man's fad' has within ten short years altered radically the whole system of modern pianoforte teaching. The Matthay Principles, Matthay Doctrines, Matthay Methods, call them what one may, are known the world over, and **probably never before in art has an almost world-wide revolution been accomplished in so short a space of time.** Truly of art did Schumann say, 'Es ist des Lernens kein Ende.'"

Crown 8vo. 4s. 6d.

THE FIRST PRINCIPLES OF PIANOFORTE PLAYING

Being an extract from the Author's "The Act of Touch." Designed for School use, and *with two additional Chapters*—"Directions for Learners and Advice to Teachers."

Crown 8vo. 2s. 6d.

COMMENTARIES
ON THE TEACHING OF PIANOFORTE TECHNIQUE.

A Supplement to "The Act of Touch" and "First Principles."

Quarto. 7s. 6d.

RELAXATION STUDIES

In the Muscular Discriminations required for Touch, Agility and Expression in Pianoforte Playing. Cloth bound (150 pages, 4to), with numerous Illustrations and Musical Examples; with a Portrait of the Author.

BOSWORTH & CO., Heddon Street, Regent Street, W.

Quarto. 1s. 6d.

THE PRINCIPLES OF FINGERING, LAWS OF PEDALLING, etc.

An Extract from above.

BOSWORTH & CO.

www.ingramcontent.com/pod-product-compliance
Lightning Source LLC
LaVergne TN
LVHW041550070426
835507LV00011B/1024